Write to the Top
A How To
for
Website Content Writing
and
Increasing Website Traffic

GREG STRANDBERG

Big Sky Words Press, Missoula

Copyright © 2013 by Big Sky Words

First paperback printing, 2015

Printed in the United States of America

All rights reserved. No part of this publication may be reproduced or transmitted in any form or by any means, electronic or mechanical, including photocopying, recording, or any information or retrieval system, without permission in writing from the publisher.

ISBN: 1508519250
ISBN-13: 978-1508519256

CONTENTS

1-Year Update — 1

Introduction — 3
Pandas, Penguins, and the Googlebot

1. Writing a Website — 6
2. Writing an About Us Page — 9
3. Writing an About Us Page: The 5 W's — 11
4. Writing an About Us Page: The Specifics — 13
5. Writing Content Pages — 16
6. Writing Content Pages: Formatting — 19
7. Writing Content Pages: The Small Things — 21
8. Writing Links — 23
9. Writing Links: Starting a Link Building Campaign — 25
10. Writing Links: Optimizing a Link Building Campaign — 28
11. Writing a Blog — 31
12. Writing a Blog: Posting Frequency — 33
13. Writing a Blog: Increasing Traffic Quickly — 36
14. Writing a Landing Page — 40
15. Writing Product Descriptions — 43
16. Writing Review Pages — 45
17. Writing an In the News Page — 48
18. Writing a Footer — 50
19. Writing a Site Map — 53

20.	Writing a Terms of Use	57
21.	Writing a Privacy Policy	62
22.	Writing a Contact Page	66
23.	Writing a FAQ	69
24.	Writing SEO	72
25.	Writing CRO	75
26.	Writing a Home Page	80
	About the Author	84

1-YEAR UPDATE

I wrote this book just about a year ago, around the time I was just starting my writing website, www.bigskywords.com.

This is a screenshot of my traffic for that first month, which was March, 2013:

Views	Top Pages (this month)	Views	Search Terms (this month)	Views	Referring Sites (this month)
274	/	2	path of the louisiana purchase	20	www.weebly.com
119	/montana-articles.html	2	bigskywords	9	www.google.com
98	/writing-articles.html	1	WWW.SKY WORDS.COM	3	whois.domaintools.com
55	/about-us.html	1	early montana explorers	3	sn142w.snt142.mail.live.com
36	/writing-samples.html			2	www.bing.com
29	/1/post/2013/03/writing-a-website			1	www.smashwords.com
28	/contact.html			1	www.google.com.au
23	/1/post/2013/03/academic-writing			1	www.freelancer.com

As you can see, I had 274 visits to my homepage that month, 9 visits from Google, and just a couple sites linking to me, hardly any of them worth much.

And the keywords people were typing in to find me? As you can see, there wasn't much.

So what did it look like around a year later, in March, 2014? Take a look:

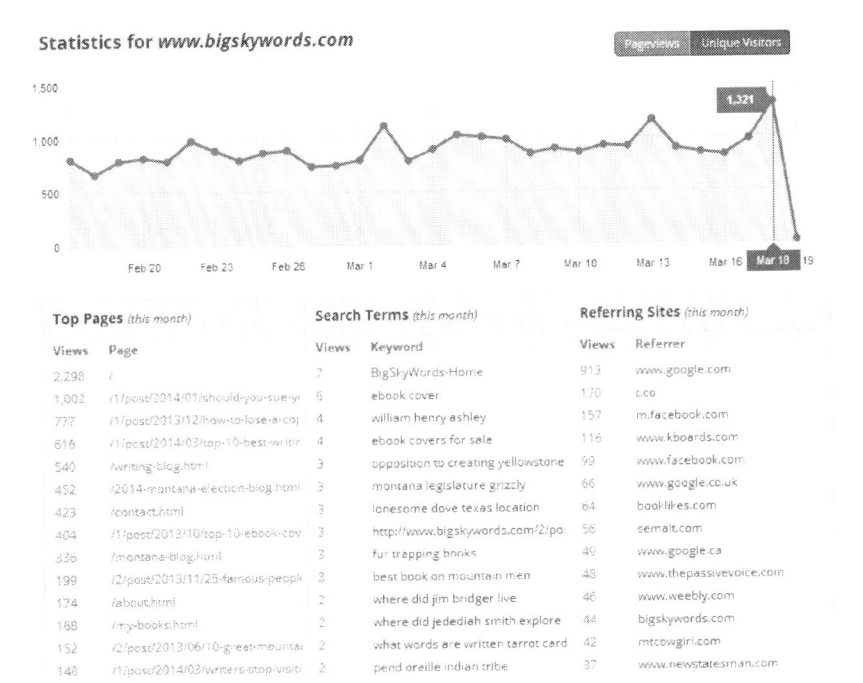

As you can see, I had 2,298 visits to my homepage, 913 visits from Google, and some big sites linking to me, many of them due to social media marketing.

And the keywords people were typing to find me? Well, I was getting targeted traffic based on my site's quality and unique content.

I'd also like to add that I did no advertising for my site, didn't use a single piece of SEO analytics software, and didn't buy a single bestselling eBook on how to increase my site's traffic.

No, I got my traffic the old fashioned way – I earned it.

Do you want your site to be doing the same in a year's time? I thought so. Read on.

INTRODUCTION
PANDAS, PENGUINS, AND THE GOOGLEBOT

The internet isn't the place it used to be. Google Panda rolled out in February 2011, and this search results ranking algorithm really leveled the playing field. Panda targeted "low quality" and "thin" sites, and nearly 12% of all search results were affected. They saw their high positions in the Search Engine Results Page (SERP) plummet, and few were able to fully recover. What was their problem? Their website's content wasn't high-quality.

Low-quality sites were still getting to the top of the rankings, however, often by means that Google didn't approve of. Google Penguin was released in April 2012 as a way to remedy this. Black-hat SEO methods, such as keyword stuffing, link schemes, and duplicate content were all targeted. 3% of existing websites were affected, bringing the total websites with low-quality content affected by the two algorithms to 15%.

In the spring of 2012 there were around 644 million websites in the world, according to Netcraft, a website hosting service based out of England. That means that Panda and Penguin had a direct effect on more than 96 million websites, lowering them in the rankings, and often ruining their business.

That's why high-quality content is so important. You don't want to be hit by Panda or Penguin, and the Googlebot will be checking. The Googlebot is a web spider or crawler that moves through those 644 million sites on the internet and indexes them. It looks at the content and indexes it in such a way that the search engine can detect the site and changes to the site. How it does this is by going through all of the links on each page of a website.

Those links lead it to other websites, and they in turn are indexed. The only way that the Googlebot will get a good look at your site is if you've got links leading to other known websites.

The best way to generate those links is to put up great content on your website and all of its pages. You want these pages written for users, not the algorithms or the search engines. You want to be up front with your users, not deceptive. Don't engage in trickery to try and bump your rankings in the search engines. Always help your users, and make your content shine and stand out from the crowd.

Those are tips that are all listed in the <u>Google Webmaster Guidelines</u> and which anyone can look at. They make it clear that the only thing that's going to get you to the top of Google is great content. Links help, but no one will link to a site with low-quality content, not with Panda and Penguin out there.

Great content is your only way to get on the first page of the Search Engine Results Page (SERP), and then to the No. 1 Page Rank. Other websites are doing it all the time, and you can too. There are several niches out there, and if you make all of your website's pages great, you'll get there. It won't happen over night, and it won't necessarily happen next week, but it will happen.

Content is king as far as Google is concerned, and we all know that Google is the king of the internet. You can make Google happy by writing great content, it's really that simple. And writing great content is easy when you know how.

This book will lay down how you can write great content for each page of your website. It details great content ideas for people just starting out on their first website, and it presents old information in a new way for those experienced with website content writing.

It discusses every aspect of making the best About Us page for your website, as well as your Product Descriptions, Review pages, and In the News pages. You'll discover how you can make those quality links with link building campaigns, and the best way to handle your blog to increase traffic quickly.

Landing pages, Site Maps, Terms of Use, Privacy Policies, Contact pages, Footers, and a FAQ will all be discussed in detail. SEO and CRO will be highlighted, and how you can make the best Home Page is explained.

So what are you waiting for? Sit down, log in, and write to the top!

1
WRITING A WEBSITE

Everyone's making a website these days, so why aren't you? The fact that you're reading this probably means that you've already decided to try your hand at writing a website. That's great, but there are many things that separate website writing from the other types of writing that you may be doing on a daily basis.

Getting your website's written content just right is important, and will elevate you in the eyes of your users, and Google. If you've done things right, once your website's up and running, you won't have to change it very often, if at all. Your great content will continue to attract new visitors, even while you sleep. So then, let's explore some ways to start in on the process.

Break it Up

I don't care if you're writing about world peace or the newest bathroom fixture; if you're not breaking up your content into easy-to-read passages, you've got some problems. Every once in a while some crazy person will publish a manifesto, and it will get some media attention. Usually the text's one long, multi-page block. Who wants to read that? Break up your content into lists, small paragraphs, or even single sentences.

Headlines

Think of reading a website like you read a newspaper. Are you delving into each topic, or just scanning the headlines for the stories that might interest you? People will do the same when they're reading your website. Make your headings and subheadings interesting, informative, and a bit flashy. And your headings will also be one of the first things the search engines look for and take note of when they index your page, so make them precisely about what your topic or content is about.

Placing your keyword into your heading is critical. Those get the most looks when Google passes by your site, and they'll help you the most when people are typing in keywords in search engines. I'm continually surprised by content out there that doesn't say what it is in the heading. Always list your keyword, both for your readers and Google.

Tone

Who are you trying to write a website for? Plumber-pants Chuck down the street, or Bill the top CEO on the block? And where do you want your website read? In the late-night dives along Skid Row, or in the executive office suites of Fortune 500 companies?

Selecting and using the right tone for your website is critical, and you've got to know who your target audience is to do that. Some things to think about are if you want to use words like "you're" or "you are." I hate the latter, and I think most CEOs do as well. Also, keep that same tone throughout your website. If the various pages of written content on your site flow smoothly and sound alike, users will have an easy time reading each of your pages.

Format

There are more formatting musts when it comes to a website besides just breaking up those large and unruly blocks of text. Consider how you want your text aligned (most websites prefer justified) as well as the spacing between sentences (one space is best for websites, two for university). Include links in your content, either through hyperlinked words right in a paragraph, or at the bottom of your page. And never forget that you can compare your website with countless others out there. Is it stealing, or just studying, when you filch ideas? And does anyone on the internet care?

When it comes to how to write a website, you'll find millions of people with the right answers. You certainly won't find all the answers here, but you will find some good pointers. And don't forget that these are not firm rules etched in stone and ready to stand the test of time. The internet changes constantly, and while the standards of writing have held for centuries, the internet doesn't necessarily have to play by those rules. If you write well, get your point across, and do both in a fun and enjoyable way for your reader, you can really do whatever you want.

2
WRITING AN ABOUT US PAGE

Who are you? Where are you? What are you doing here? Why do you exist?

These are all questions that people coming to your website on a regular basis, or even for the very first time, will be asking of you. But they're not going to waste their time writing an email with their inquiries. Instead they're going to find the information they want from your website, or move on to another. So why not make it easy for them to learn about you by writing a detailed and informative, yet concise and entertaining, About Us page?

I've written dozens of About Us pages for different websites from all around the world. Some people want every conceivable thing imaginable under the sun listed on their About Us page, even if that makes the page thousands of words long and a huge scroll.

Some people are happy with just the basics, a few hundred words if even that. And nearly all of them have no idea how they want their About Us page formatted to tell the user what they want to know quickly, efficiently, and without a lot of hassle.

You can divide the people who look at your About Us page into one of three categories:

Visitors

These people probably got to your website from a search engine, or maybe a link in an email. Word of mouth could also have propelled them to you, or even a media mention or ad campaign. However they got there, they're here now. You have a great opportunity to turn this first-timer into a regular user if your About Us page is compelling and informative.

Users

People that come to your site on a daily or weekly basis are your regular users, and they'll form the backbone of your site's internet traffic. At some point, perhaps after a few days and perhaps as long as a few months, they'll decide they want to find out more about who you are. By this time they probably already have a good idea based on your site's content and services. Your About Us page therefore needs to explain specific information without coming across as too specialized or difficult.

Customers

If you've got a great site up and running, it's only a matter of time before people begin seeking you out for work-related matters or to make purchases. These could be companies that want to place advertising on your site, someone that wants to put their similar product on your site, or even researchers who want to take snippets or even entire posts from your blog.

Every customer you get at your e-commerce site will start out as a visitor before turning into a user and customer. Before I buy a product from a site I always take a quick look at the site's About Us page, and you should too. Not every customer will do so, of course, but many that go to your site will, and if they don't like what they see, they'll not be spending their hard-earned dollars with you.

Customers are ready to give you money, and they'll be looking for detailed information about you to ease their fears. People on the internet can be anyone they say they are, but few are really who or what they claim. Your About Us page needs to allay these fears, while also enticing people to give you money or use your services.

There are many easy things you can do with your About Us page, and you might find that it becomes one of the most popular pages on your whole site as a result. Experiment at lot. Find what works, and what doesn't. An About Us page can change and evolve along with your site, just as your visitors, users, and customers are doing in their daily lives.

3
WRITING AN ABOUT US PAGE
THE 5 W's

Once you know the three main groups of people that will be visiting your About Us page, visitors, users, and customers, you can begin targeting your About Us page directly to them.

When I write About Us pages I like to break the page into 3 to 4 main sections: About Us, Features, Services, and sometimes The Difference.

In the first section, which I simply call "About Us," I break everything about the business or website down into some basic questions, or 5 W's: Who, What, Where, When, Why.

Who

Use the name of your business or website right away, and often. Just because someone is on your site doesn't mean that they know the name of it. Many people follow links from search engines or emails and wind up not on your home page, but on some random page of your website. Make them remember who you are by repeating it enough so they remember, but not so often to turn them off.

What

You want to tell people what you can do for them right away, in your About Us page's first section. This is where you can really push into the clouds, and let people dream big. You want to tug on people's emotions, and get them to feel they need whatever it is you're offering.

Where

This is pretty easy. If you're a physical business just getting onto the internet, simply put down your physical location, like 1400 First Street, Podunk, USA. If you're offering digital goods or services on your site, tell them about where you live, and what it's like. "For 3 years we've been operating out of the beautiful Round Building on First Street, Podunk, USA." They're really the same thing, and if you want visitors to become regular users who trust your site, tell them where you're at.

One note: if you're going to be putting up a Contact page on your site, you can save a lot of these details for there. You don't want to be repeating yourself on different pages of your site. Users don't like duplicate content, and Google hates it.

When

How long have you been operating, and why did you start are some good things to touch upon in this section. If you started your website just a month ago, why not go into detail on when you began thinking about helping other people? If you've been operating a physical business but are just getting onto the internet, tell people about your years of experience. Dates and times will give you and your website a more personalized feel for people visiting for the first time, or even regularly. And when things are more personal, they'll trust you more, and buy from you.

Why

Tell people why you have a website. One of the main reasons is that you probably want to make money, but you shouldn't grab your bull horn and start shouting this to the heavens. Tell people about how you had a job that made you realize how much you could help others. Let visitors know about your frustrations over an existing product, and how your product alleviates those frustrations. Explain that you couldn't find the perfect ringtone to save your life unless you spent 3 hours going back-and-forth between various sites, and you want to make everything take less time by putting it all in one spot. While your main goal may be to make money, you also want to help people, and that's the angle you need to push.

4
WRITING AN ABOUT US PAGE
THE SPECIFICS

Now that you've touched upon the 5 W's of your business or website, you need to get into specifics.

- What features does your website have that separates it from all the others out there?

- What services do you offer, and how do your features make these services better?

- And what is the overall difference between you and your competitors.

If you can give specifics for each of these points, you'll be well on your way to a great About Us page.

Features

This is the section where you want to set yourself apart from all the other websites out there that offer the same services as you do. What makes you different, but more importantly, what makes you better? Features are not given to your customers; they instead make the things you do give to your customers so much better.

Let's say you have a potato peeler. Some of the features of this potato peeler are its smooth design, easy-grip handle, and ice-hardened steel edge that won't require sharpening. This is what sets your potato peeler apart from the thousands on the market today.

If your About Us page is for a hotel, talk about how the rooms are better than the competitors in the area, and give specifics in bulleted points. I wrote an About Us page for a hotel in Bali, Indonesia, and talked a lot about the different waterfalls they had around the pool and the feng shui designs in the rooms. Those features set that hotel apart from others in the area.

Another About Us page I worked on was for auto repair shops. I listed all of the great equipment they had in their garage, even if everyone else in town had the same tools. Other features were the 1400 square foot repair facility, their attention to detail, and their certificate saying they were a State Certified Emission Repair Facility.

I had to go around to many different websites when I was writing a series of About Us page templates for a company making custom websites for auto repair shops. I was continually amazed at how many sites didn't list what they did for customers, or did so in a hard-to-read way. You want to make your information easy to understand, quick to read, and short. People visiting your About Us page probably won't read every single sentence, but they will scan the main points, so make these shine.

Services

This is different from features in a few key ways. Services are things that are offered to your customers, features are ways that those services can be offered and delivered better than your competitors. The features of your business or website are what set you apart from your competitors. The services you offer are things that people can buy. These are often physical things, or perhaps a digital good. Either way, they're something that you deliver.

When I was writing about the Bali hotel, I talked about the features that set them apart from other hotels in the area. In the services section I talked about airport shuttle services, concierge services, and a 24-hour security watch. Even something simple can be a service, like the coffee machine in the room. "All of our rooms are stocked with gourmet coffee from Peru, making your mornings so much more brighter." While that coffee was probably made months ago and is in a paper pouch from a box, it's still something you're giving the customer.

Services that the auto repair shop offered were electrical systems diagnostics, full transmission flushes, and tire rotations and alignments. I listed about 15 different services in bulleted points so that users could quickly scan the list and find what they were looking for. I made each item on the list link to an area of the website that would give detailed information for that particular service, making the user-experience easier and more efficient.

The Difference

There are hundreds of hotels in Bali and dozens of auto repair shops in your area. Why should I choose you?

The Difference section of your About Us page needs to be the clincher that convinces people that you are right for them. Sometimes I see this labeled as the "Why Choose Us?" section as well. No matter what you call it, this is your final sell, and more than any other section of your About Us page, you want to tug on the visitors emotions. Use empathy, and make them trust you. Identify with their problems and needs, and explain how you've been there before. Here are two examples:

Bali Hotel

You've been dreaming of taking that great holiday vacation to Bali for years now, and it looks like it will really happen this time. You're checking flights, pulling the suitcases out of the garage, and looking at the kids' summer schedule. You've already put so much time into planning your great holiday vacation, so why not choose the best hotel you can? Bali Hotel cares about you and your family and we'll give you the best accommodations on the island. Our years of service prove this, and our customers all agree: Bali Hotel is your best choice this holiday season!

Auto Repair Shop

You've experienced poor service before, and seen the prices on even the most common of repair jobs go through the roof. At Podunk Auto, all of our costs are up-front, and there aren't any hidden fees. Our employees are our family, and our customers our friends. And friends don't shortchange you for a quick buck. We want a long and healthy relationship with you, and that's why our team of certified professionals work tirelessly to make sure your auto repair job is done right and on time, the very first time you come in our door. So don't settle for second-best ever again, choose Podunk Auto for all your repair and service needs.

5
WRITING CONTENT PAGES

- Boring and basic;
- Slow and sorrowful;
- Lazy and lethargic;
- Crummy and crude;
- Out-of-touch and out-of-date;
- Prosaic and pitiful.

You'll have several different pages of content on your website. And you want none of them to be described as that. What you do want is for:

Each one of these content pages to be unique, even if they're all pretty much saying the same thing;

Each one of these content pages to be interesting and informative;

And each one of these content pages to look good.

People reading on the web tend to read slower than average, or at least that's what websites on 'writing a website' will all claim. I also hear that people who read on the web are a bit finicky as well. So you might need to change the way you write normally. When you're writing a website, it's therefore important to consider a few things to make you stand out.

– **Short and Sweet**: People reading websites don't read much. They skip about a lot. And they look for main points. Keep things simple, short, and to the point.

— **Readability**: Make your website's written content easy to read. Break it up into blocks. Keep the sentences short. Make it look good.

— **Headlines**: Make the key information stand out. Give strong headings that make sense. Use subheadings that are easy to read and easy to find. Tell everything in as few words as possible; it's the most that people will read anyways.

— **Bite the Bullet**: You might want to put everything into big blocks, but don't. Use bulleted lists, and use them frequently. But don't overuse them.

— **Links**: Always open a link in a new window. Why would you want people having to hit 'back' when they go to your linked site? It's easier if all links open up a new tab on your visitor's browser, making it easier to get back to you.

— **Scrolling**: People have mouse scroll balls and laptop scroll pads. And they use them to good effect. Break things up, give them a heading, and don't get scrolled out of town.

— **Be Up-Front**: Don't save the best for last when it comes to writing a website. Give your best information right at the top of your page, and say it loud and clear. Put the boring stuff last.

Now, if you were reading this on a website, I'd expect that you would have made it this far down the page. I've used bulleted lists, and I tried like hell to grab the reader's attention right from the get-go. So now I can go back and write like I usually do, right?

Perhaps. That's why there's no formula for writing a great website content page. Websites change everyday, and the best site from last year is done and gone, at least if they've got the same old boring content. Things happen quickly on the web, and information is spreading and changing all the time. If you can hook people in, give them good information throughout your content page, and then get them to the end, that's your handle.

Use your final bit of content to really reel them in. You've got them this far, now how can you convince them that everything you just said was factual, made sense, and wasn't a legitimate waste of their time?

You can't. Your content has already spoken for you. Anything you say now will just be redundant. So go back and make what you said earlier, better. That's what website content writing is all about, after all, the continual process of change. Bit of a bummer, huh?

6
WRITING CONTENT PAGES FORMATTING

How many websites do you go to each day? Probably quite a few. There are your regular websites for news, weather, sports, as well as your favorite interests and hobbies. But there are also plenty of websites that you visit each day that are new and unknown to you. What kind of impression do they make?

- Is the **relevant information** you're looking for presented right at the top of the page? Or do you have to scroll all the way to the bottom to find what you're looking for?

- Do the **headings and subheadings** tell you everything you need to know? Or are you digging through the blocky paragraphs looking for what you seek?

- Most people that surf the internet regularly will come across many new sites each day, and they'll determine how useful that site is to them in a matter of seconds. It's not just what the content says, but **how it's presented**.

- If I'm looking for a cooking recipe, I'll be much more inclined to stay on the page with **easy-to-read text, bulleted points, and a nice picture** of what I want to eat.

- If I find a cooking recipe with all of the text the same size, no real heading, and everything in one long sentence stretching across the page, **I'll immediately close out that tab or window on my browser**, or hit back like my life depended upon it.

Just take a look at how all of the above information looks when it's unformatted:

6 Writing Content Pages: Formatting
How many websites do you go to each day? Probably quite a few. There are your regular websites for news, weather, sports, your favorite interests and hobbies. But there are also plenty of websites that you visit each day that are new and unknown to you. What kind of impression do they make? Is the relevant information you're looking for presented right at the top of the page? Or do you have to scroll all the way to the bottom to find what you're looking for? Do the headings and subheadings tell you everything you need to know? Or are you digging through the blocky paragraphs looking for what you seek? Most people that surf the internet regularly will come across many new sites each day, and they'll determine how useful that site is to them in a matter of seconds. It's not just what the content says, but how it's presented. If I'm looking for a cooking recipe, I'll be much more inclined to stay on the page with easy-to-read text, bulleted points, and a nice picture of what I want to eat. If I find a cooking recipe with all of the text the same size, no real heading, and everything in one long sentence stretching across the page, I'll immediately close out that tab or window on my browser, or hit back like my life depended upon it.

Well?

If you saw that, what would you do? You'd hit back and wonder about the fool who put it up, that's what you'd do! So don't make the mistake that thousands of websites out there are doing, and use formatting for your website's content pages. Please!

7
WRITING CONTENT PAGES
THE SMALL THINGS

I write a lot of website content, thousands of words of it each day. I control how that content looks when I put it up on my own websites, but I don't always have a say in how others use the content I write for them.

Either way, I try to give my content a certain look before I even put it up on my webpage. That's right! I'm not writing this content on the webpage where it will show up, I'm writing it in MS Word, either right before I post it, or perhaps even days or weeks in advance.

You have a lot more power and freedom when you aren't writing on your webpage, and some great tools. Let's look at some ways to write content off-page, and touch upon all of the small things in the process.

Bullets

Don't bother with bullets when you're writing your website's content in MS Word. Lots of the time when you go to copy/paste the content onto your webpage, the bullets won't transfer well. I always just separate the bulleted information with a few returns. I also know all of the bulleted points before hand, usually because I have one main word at the start of each bullet block.

Copy/Paste

When you write your website content pages in MS Word, or any other word processing application, you have the power to just copy and paste it right onto your webpage. This is great when you've got a lot of ideas for your content one day, but you might not want to put it up right away. Many blogs allow you to save drafts which you can publish at later date. This saves a lot of hassles each day, so set an hour aside each week to upload drafts.

Saving

You can save your content in MS Word, and you can also get the exact word count. A good rule of thumb for website SEO content is to have a minimum of 500 words. If you can continually check where you're at, it will make a big difference in how much, and how fast you can write.

Retrieval

When you write your website content off-site, you're saving it on your computer. It's a lot easier to go back and look at old posts if you don't have to scroll through them all, or follow the links. Believe me, when you get up past 100 posts, you'll appreciate seeing them all in a Windows folder.

Pictures

I wouldn't even focus on pictures when you're writing your website's content pages. I always have an idea of what pictures I'll use when I'm writing, but I won't go and retrieve those, either through finding them on the internet or getting them from my computer, until I've completely finished writing. And then I'll put the writing up first before I insert the pictures.

Captions

Another thing that I often see missing from website content pages are captions. When I see a picture, I want to know what it is right away; I don't wan to have to dig through the text for a description. Put up a simple, to-the-point caption, and make sure it's only a few words, or at most a very short sentence.

8
WRITING LINKS

I call it 'you rub my back, I'll rub yours.' That's in essence what a link building strategy is. And that's exactly the kind of strategy, of helping others so they'll help you, that you want when you're writing links for your website.

Every time your website accepts an incoming link, or creates and outgoing link, it creates a little 'ping' on the internet. This signals the search engines that hey, there's some action there, and we better look. The more action you get, the more popular you'll be, just like in high school.

There are many ways to go about getting that linking action, and a link building campaign is a great place to start. So let's get right into some of the basics.

Content

If you've got good content, people will link to you. Let's take as an example Mount Itshuey. Have you heard of it? No? Neither have I! Then why is everyone talking about it? We have to search it out!

If you've got great content about something that people want to know about, like Mount Itshuey, then you'll get bumped up in the Search Engine Results Page (SERP) real quick. Other websites that are in any way related to Mount Itshuey will want to piggyback on you by having a link to your site. It's a two-way street, so if there's great content about the new restaurant on Mount Itshuey that you didn't even know about, and it's on someone else's site, you better link to it quick!

Competitors

Knowing what your enemies are doing, oh sorry, competitors, is vital for a successful link building campaign. If you've got a website devoted to Mount Itshuey, then you need to search for that keyword and find the other sites devoted to it. Search their pages and take note of all the links they have listed, or even copy them into a separate document for perusal later.

You're going to want to go to those links as well, when you have time, to find out how you can make your site's content better, and also how you can draw the traffic away from those competitors. What are they doing that you're not? Do they have more keywords sprinkled about their content than you do? Those are some questions you want to ask yourself when you start looking at your competitors. And don't discount linking to them; remember if you help them, they'll help you, whether they want to or not.

Counts

Most people will tell you that a page with too many links is a problem. Experts say that linking to a page with a few links is better than linking to a page with lots of links. I'm not so sure about this, and I think even the experts will admit the jury's out on that one.

I have an ESL website, esladventure.com, and my most popular page is my ESL Links page. I get hundreds of hits on that page each month, and it brings me no profit, but lots of traffic to my site, and other pages on my site. I have about 45 links to other ESL sites, and they're all quality links. That's the handle. Linking to a lot of quality links is better than linking to a few rubbish links, and vice versa.

9
WRITING LINKS
STARTING A LINK BUILDING CAMPAIGN

Links can be what hold us together, or tear us apart. Great links on a website will get you noticed by other websites. Bad links on sites will get you dinged by the search engines and drive down traffic to your site.

So how do you know what's good and what's bad? You've got to put in a lot of legwork on the internet finding relevant, useful, and quality links. That takes time, and it takes even longer for the search engines to notice what you've done.

The word campaign by its very nature implies a large undertaking, and large undertakings take time, months or years in fact. When you embark on a new link building campaign, don't expect results tomorrow, next week, or maybe even in a month. You'll see a trickle of new traffic, but if you stick to your guns, that trickle will turn into a torrent over time.

Ranking

You've got to consider not only your Page Rank when you begin a link building campaign, but the Page Rank of your competitors, those that you are linking to, and those that are linking to you. Page Rank is actually PageRank, named after Google's Larry Page who came up with the search engine's algorithm. It's where you come up when people type a keyword into Google, and the higher you are, the more people will see you.

Linking to your competitors and having them link to you is good. That sounds like a lot to consider, but just think of it like this: your website will do so much better if websites with high Page Ranks link to you, as opposed to websites with low Page Ranks.

A link from thewashingtonpost.com is a lot better than a link from carlsmom.com, so consider this when you're choosing your links. But what do you do when someone like Carl's mom links to you? You really don't want that if you're planning on making a successful site.

Links that are from inferior websites, websites that exist in a type of ether on the internet, never getting any new content, never getting any visitors, and never really seeing the warm glow of a computer screen again just won't help you. You don't want that, but there's not much you can do about it. There are no link police on the internet after all, unless you count the googlebot.

Anchoring

Anchor text is what your links look like when they don't look like html. This is how my website appears – http://www.bigskywords.com. The problem is that it just doesn't look that good. How about this instead – Big Sky Words. It looks a little better, doesn't it?

Now let's take the example one step further, and show how anchor text can improve your Page Rank. My website has a lot of writing and history articles on it, so let's say that I want to link to the best way to write a website's links without really trying. A lot of people would probably be interested in how that particular sentence fragment sounds, so they'd click on it. And the search engines like it because it's got a few good keywords in there, like 'write a website' and 'website's links.'

Both will get good hits. But it looks good too, is fully part of the paragraph, and tells the search engines what your link is about. All three of those links go back to the same spot, but only one of them looks the best, has keywords in it, and tells the user exactly what the link is. That is how you want to use anchor text.

Baiting

There's nothing wrong with link baiting, at least as far as the search engines are concerned. Link baiting is when you put content up on your site with the intention of drawing in links from other sites.

Videos and pictures are a great example. We've all seen or heard about cute kitten or puppy videos that get tens of thousands of hits. Other websites link to that site so that they can get more traffic themselves.

How about a funny photo of someone with their head stuck in something? The way social media is these days, people will be flocking to the picture and sharing it with their friends. Everyone will go back to the site that has the content. So if you can find something hilarious, shocking, or just downright wrong, put it up on your site or link to it; you never know, it might be the best thing you ever did for your website.

10
WRITING LINKS
OPTIMIZING A LINK BUILDING CAMPAIGN

So you've made the decision to start a link building campaign, now how do you go about doing it? First you need to figure out what the quality links related to your website are. Make sure the links you choose to put up on your site help your user. Don't focus so much on how many links you have, just how good they are. And don't get caught up in any link schemes that will just penalize you in the long run.

Quality Links

Only link to quality sites. So what are quality sites? Sites that get a lot of traffic could be considered quality sites, but not all sites getting a lot of traffic are quality sites that you want to be affiliated with, or send your visitors toward.

Government sites are a great place to link to, as they'll provide trusted information that is useful. Your largest competitor, be it Amazon or CNN, will also be a good choice for your links, as they're reputable and again, provide quality and useful information.

The important thing to remember is that you don't want to be linking to sites that don't have anything to do with your content. While sending visitors on to that cute puppy video might make their day, it won't do much for you in the eyes of Google, and could even hurt you.

Help Your User

Another important question to ask yourself when you put those links on your site is, "Will this help my user?" Of course, to answer that question you have to know who your users are. You should be able to figure that out by studying your sites analytics and scanning the keywords that get directed to your site. Those are people that are looking for something related to whatever content you have now.

Search out those keywords yourself and find out what other sites pop up. If they're good, and I mean really good, link to them. If you have a site with 52 Tabasco sauce recipes, and you find a different site with 367, then you should link to it. In the meantime, figure out how you can come up with 368 recipes.

Does Size Count?

How many links do you need to have the most successful link building campaign? I don't know. There's no clear answer on that, but again, Google recommends that you prioritize quality over quantity. That doesn't mean you can't have a lot of links.

The most popular page on my ESL website esladventure.com is the Links Page. I put this page up pretty quickly after I set up my website because I wanted to help other ESL teachers that had struggled like I once did.

I have 45 links on the page, each of them grouped under different headings like pronunciation, grammar, games, word searches, coloring pages, and so on. Each link also has a short description under it telling the user what is on that site and how it can help them.

I knew all of the links were good because I had used all of them to aid me in the classroom, and had compiled them in a list. Before I put them up on my site I made sure they were all still going to the place I wanted them to, and I check them periodically. If a link is heading to a dead end, I'll remove it right away. Pointing to links that head to any 300 or 400-level redirect sites are not what you want.

My main concern when I put them up was not increasing the traffic to my site, and I could have cared less about increasing the traffic to the other sites. I just knew that there was some quality information and resources that I wasn't supplying, and had no intention of supplying. All I wanted to do was help my user. That is the kind of attitude that will give your website some real staying power on the internet.

I also knew that those sites, if they were on top of their game, would be studying their analytics. They would see that some of their traffic, probably a small amount at first, was coming from esladventure.com. There's a good chance that they would have gone to my site, checked it out, and if they liked what they saw, they'd make a link to me. So by helping my user as much as I can, even by linking to a competitor, I'm in the end helping myself.

Link Schemes

Google defines a 'link scheme' as "Any links intended to manipulate a site's ranking in Google search results" and it violates their <u>Webmaster Guidelines</u>. They see it as trying to manipulate their search results, they don't like that, and they'll ding you accordingly. I've worked with some people who've tried such black-hat SEO methods, and they've all told me that they're trying to dig themselves out of the hole they created for themselves by doing that. Some of them had high a high Page Rank until the googlebot spotted them and lowered them considerably in the rankings.

It takes quite awhile sometimes for the googlebot to pass by your site again to see if you've changed your ways, and you'll be struggling to catch up until then. It's best not to even let that happen in the first place by only using quality links that are directly related to your content.

Google says in their Webmaster Guidelines that the best way to ensure you'll have quality links coming in to your site is by creating the best and most useful content that you can. You've got to find out what your biggest competitors are doing with their content, and you've got to make it a whole lot better. Your content needs to create a buzz, and increasingly that buzz will come from the various social networking sites and applications being used today. Nothing sells like word of mouth.

11
WRITING A BLOG

Posting is a process that takes time, if done right. You can slap up just about any old content onto your site, but why would you want to? Your readers won't appreciate it, and the search engines won't either. You'll end up feeling quite lonely, and no website wants that.

There's more to posting than just writing something informative and meaningful; you've also got to think long-term about how you want those posts to benefit your site.

Are you posting for fun, or as a way to increase your online business? Do your posts have a unified and linear structure that makes sense, or are they just thrown up haphazardly with no thought as to how long they'll be there, how many people will read them, or how much electronic dust they'll collect?

That's why it's so important to have an overall and long-term blog posting strategy, and you can start that by asking yourself three simple questions.

How Often Am I Posting?

If you're like me you'll put up one article a day. 5 to 7 a week is therefore no problem. I think posting any more than that is not necessary, and simply becomes unsustainable after time. What do you do when you get up to 30 posts after a few weeks and you run out of ideas?

You want to make sure you go at a pace that is good for you as a writer or poster, and for the search engines. They only need one a day, after all. Instead of posting more than that each week, sit down and write out an outline for the month. It'll make it so much easier to add content to your website long-term.

What's My Theme?

If you've made an outline of what your monthly blog posts will be, you'll see a theme begin to form. If you've got a good theme to your posts, they'll all tie together. And if you can tie all of your posts together, you can put them into an eBook.

More and more sites these days are putting eBooks up for sale or as free giveaways. It's a great marketing tool for your site, and a way to earn a little extra income. Income, I might add, that is all passive, and which can come to you for years after you've done all the work.

You can see from my own site bigskywords.com that many of my posts have similar titles. This works well for people using search engines, and it also works good for me when I go to make them into an eBook.

Am I Link Building?

If you're not hard at work on a link building campaign for your website, you're way behind the curve. The sites coming up to the top of the Search Engine Results Page (SERP) will often have many incoming links, as well as outgoing links. You'll need both to stay competitive over time, and that's why it's so important to include links with all of your posts.

You might think that you're giving the competition a leg up, and that's true. But you're also sending a message to that site telling it you exist, as well as the search engines that note the connection. Both will cause your traffic to increase. And if enough traffic is coming from your site to a competitor or similar site, they'll take not, and eventually include a link to you as well.

12
WRITING A BLOG POSTING FREQUENCY

'Post and post often' is a common expression when it comes to the question of how often you should put up new content on your website. But how often is often, and how often is too often? There are a few things you should consider when it comes to the frequency of your posts, and what you want those posts to do for your website.

Make it New

People will come to your website if it has quality content, and if that content changes frequently. Just like people pick up a newspaper to see what's changed from one day to the next, so too will people visit your website if they know the content will be new and fresh each day. Therefore posting once a day is a must.

When you put up new content on your website, and especially blog posts, people will know. Many times you can create an email list that will send out a notification to those who've signed up. They've done that because they like what you're content's saying.

These are people who want to read each and every new post that you've got, meaning you're doing a great job! Every time you post, they'll get an email, and you'll get another visitor. But even regular visitors will turn away if no new content is available.

Posting for Growth

A posting strategy works with whatever goals you have for your website. If you want to grow like crazy, and you've got the ability to create fresh and exciting content each day, post 3 to 5 different times each day. There are plenty of people willing to write articles and blog posts for your site, if you pay them of course. And many of them will even put that content right up on your website for you, reducing your need to do much of anything.

If you want steady, long-term growth you should post everyday. You've only got to pump out 500 words or so, and can even do less on days when you're just not feeling up to it. The key is posting each and everyday, however. And it's not as hard as it sounds; seeing how many blog posts your website begins to accrue will be a great motivator for you to continue.

Always read through any comments your blog or other content is getting, and reply quickly. Someone who left a comment is waiting to hear back from you, and the faster you deliver, and the more personalized you make each comment, will both ensure that you've just gone a long way in creating a dedicated user of your website. And don't be afraid to comment on other websites that are similar to yours. Just make sure you put a link to your own website's content in the comment or your user account.

Posting for Fun

If you're not concerned about growing your site and increasing your users, post less frequently. A couple of posts each week, or even a few quality posts each month will still have you adding great content. If you've got a very specialized website with unique content that's sought after in your niche, you'll have people checking you out.

You might not see your traffic increase a whole lot when you're not posting that often, but at least you'll still be in the game. And perhaps you just want to make your views known, or just get them into the computer and out of your head. A blog post is a great way to do both.

Whether you're posting for fun or as a serious way to drive up the traffic to your site, always make sure you're comfortable. If you find yourself getting behind on posts when you thought you'd be putting up new content each day, slow down and figure out what you can do. Oftentimes just writing the titles down that you want to talk about each week will go a long way.

Also consider having several smaller-sized articles or posts that you can throw up on those days that you just feel yourself dragging. Nothing's better than putting up an article you wrote the day before, and having a much needed rest. If you're putting up 30 articles each month, you'll need it!

13
WRITING A BLOG
INCREASING TRAFFIC QUICKLY

Everyone wants to get their website's blog right to the top of Google. Many try, but the sad truth is that very few succeed. It's tough getting to the top, and once your there everyone wants to knock you off, claiming that spot for themselves. It's a precarious position, and few find they can be the 'king of the hill' for long.

There are many things you can do that will move your blog posts up in the rankings, and you don't have to spend a lot of time slaving away at your computer to do them. Simple things like making email subscriber lists, enabling social networking access, posting on forums in your niche, and commenting on likeminded blogs are all ways to see you boost the traffic to your blog. You'll also increase the validity of your posts, and your relevance to Google, as well as all those using it to find what they need.

Email Lists

You've got to let people know when you're putting up your content. It's rather sadistic to slave away at a computer writing great content if no one's going to read it. Still, many people do just that everyday, at least as far as the traffic to their site is concerned.

If you're a J.D. Salinger-type who likes to keep their best stuff under lock and key, then go ahead, collect that internet dust. But if you want people that have read your stuff before to know that you've got new stuff out there, let them subscribe to a list that notifies them by email each time you add new content.

Social Networking

I always discounted the importance of social media because I lived in China for so long. You can't use Facebook there unless you've got a VPN, and even then your access could be spotty at best. YouTube has been banned since 2008 in the Middle Kingdom, and Twitter is thought of as a way to share information and bring people together, something the Chinese authorities dread.

So I never enabled my FaceBook, Twitter, and RSS Feeds, and I never saw a lot of traffic on my site as a result. Boy, was I making a big error of judgment; just as big as the Chinese were making by not allowing this great source of traffic, and possibly income, to flow in. Do yourself a favor, and let the world onto your site by enabling social networking.

Forum Posting

Forum posting is a hassle, and it may take away from what your trying to do with your own blog, namely get a post onto it each day or each week. If you're writing on someone else's website, after all, you're not writing on your own.

Still, thousands of people are going to forums, and you and your site could do with the exposure. Find out what forums are talking about your niche, and start reading what people are saying.

You don't need to write a lengthy treatise, and you certainly don't need to make posts everyday. What you should do is occasionally scroll through the most recent posts to see what is relevant to you and your site, and comment accordingly. People will read and listen, and if you're good, they'll want to find out what you'll say next.

Commenting

Make sure that you find your competition's blog. Go to the sites that you most want to be like, or whose content you like the most. Sign up for their email list, and each time there's a new post, write a comment. Put a link back to your site in the comment or your user account, or just mention your site's name. After enough of those types of comments you'll have a lot of validity.

The key is making sure that you're putting quality comments out onto those other sites, and not a lot of garbage. If you just put one sentence, like "I like it!" followed by a link to your site, people won't take you seriously. That type of 'robo-commenting' is considered as spam, and may actually hurt you in the long run.

Now, if you can get onto 10 blog email lists, and stay up with their posts while still posting your own content, you'll quickly see a boost in traffic. The key is to keep making your own posts, and not just spending your time contributing to someone else's. Finding a right balance between your posting frequency, and the marketing involved with your posting, is therefore critical, and a necessary step on the long road to the top of Google.

Reference Other Posts

Putting a link to another post at the bottom of your own post, or within it through anchor text is a great idea. But you can take it a step further by talking about the other blog post as well. Tell about how you read a great blog post on increasing traffic from so-and-so, and how their 7 key ideas really made you think differently about your own website.

If you can talk about a great article, and give a link to it, it will increase your own relevance in your regular users' eyes, and those that just happened to stumble upon your post.

One great post that I used when writing this was 21 Tactics to Increase Blog Traffic on SEOMoZ. This post is great for a variety of reasons.

It has a great title, with a number displayed prominently. Whenever I'm searching for Google, I'll always click on the title with a large number. It might not give me the best content, but it will give me a lot of keywords that I can think about, and write my own content around.

All 21 points are formatted well, and each contains a wonderful graphic. They range from large graphs to actual website screenshots. Pictures always say more than your content can, and people like their text broken up by them.

Analytics are shown and discussed, with arrows pointing to what's being talked about. Take note of those and see if you can begin looking at your own site's analytics more analytically.

The article is on one page, not 21 pages that I have to click through. By listing more pages you might be getting more page views, and perhaps more advertising opportunities. I think it's a bad tactic, however. I hate waiting to transfer between all of those pages, and I'll usually go somewhere else pretty quickly, unless the content is good. Remember, if you've got great content, you can do just about anything.

There's a huge comment section on this page, and you can learn a lot by just reading those. Sometimes I'll go to a site and read the blog post, scroll down the page, and find I've learned more from the other bloggers who commented. Don't neglect what those long pages of comments tell you; they probably hold quite a few secrets on what works when it comes to blogging, and what doesn't.

14
WRITING A LANDING PAGE

Your website's landing page is often the first thing a visitor to your site will see. What you have on your landing page could keep them interested, or turn them away.

The only reason you have anyone on your landing page anyway is because they clicked on a search engine link that brought them there. Something they typed into Google brought up a string of results, and one of the results that appeared was an ad to your site. That's right; your ad campaigns bring people to your landing page. They clicked on the link, and were brought to your landing page.

Now the question is what are you going to do to keep them interested? How are you going to get them to look around your site, click on your advertisements, and maybe even buy one of your products? You're going to get them interested, and keep them interested, by having great landing page content. Let's take a look at how you can go about getting that.

Make it Short

When someone clicks on a link to get to your website, it means they're surfing around. You've got to pull them in quick, or they'll jump to the next link down on the Search Engine Results Page (SERP). Give them a quick, easy to see paragraph or two, perhaps in bullet points and with hyperlinked text, which tells them what they're looking for.

How do you know what they're looking for? Because you've SEO'd your site to such an extent that you've pulled them in. You'll also be able to check your analytics, either on your own site or with things like Google Analytics and Google Adsense, to see what keywords these visitors are using.

One of the keywords that you used somewhere got their attention and now they're reading your content. Your landing page therefore needs content that shows those keywords loud and clear, and within a few seconds. If people don't see what they're looking for in that amount of time, they'll go somewhere else. If you want to make them a regular visitor, or a satisfied customer, you've got to sell it to them fast.

Make it Sweet

Make sure you're clear on what your landing page's intention is, and make sure your visitor is clear as well. Use big text, do what you can to draw attention to it, but please state your goal, service, or product that you're pushing.

If you're goal is to post great blog content about wheelbarrows and the myriad attachments that go with them, make that clear in your headlines and short supporting paragraph.

If your service is 1,001 Fun, Amazing, Exciting, and Mind-Blowing English Classroom Games, all for the low prices of $9.99/month, put it right at the top of your page and with and eye-catching image nearby.

And if you're product is "The Best Damned Toenail Clippers This Side of the Mississippi!" well, by all means, state it loud and clear and put a picture of them there too.

Remember, if you've written your ad content well, it gives the users a taste of what you're offering. Their appetites have been whetted and they're looking for more. By pulling them in with that ad you've fulfilled the function of your ad campaign, which you are paying for. Don't let that money go to waste by not converting this visitor to a user or customer. You've sold them this far, now take them all the way.

More about this is talked of in the chapter on Conversion Rate Optimization (CRO), but the basics are pretty simple: write clear, concise content with a strong call to action. This visitor needs something, they want to buy it, and you're selling it. Don't bombard them with more ads and don't waste their time with paragraphs of content. Less is more when it comes to your landing page, and this is your opportunity to make yourself shine in a few lines or less.

Make it to the Point

The point of your landing page is to get visitors to what is the point of your website, your content or products. You don't want people spending a lot of time on your landing page.

Think of it as a busy runway at the airport. Planes are constantly taking off and landing, and one can't be sitting there for too long. You've got to get them moving on to their destination, which in this case is your blog, products page, or shopping cart. The landing page drew them in, but now you've got to send your visitors to where they can help you the most.

That means you need to have your content quite short, and you've got to have links, preferably through anchor text. Put that within your content so that visitors can get to the pages you want them to go to, and which they want to go to. Don't let someone read a lot on your landing page. Don't clutter it up with a lot of written content, or pictures. If they like what they see on your landing page, they'll click onto your other pages, and you need to help them do that.

You'll help them immensely if you put a Buy Now or Checkout button on your landing page. If you're running a well-oiled ad campaign, you'll have several different advertisements, perhaps for several different products. Each of those advertisements should have its own landing page. You can put a great picture and description of the product up, and a link leading to the purchase screen. You don't need a whole lot more than that.

In all of my time searching around thousands of different sites doing content writing work for people, I've enjoyed seeing simple sites more than complicated ones. A great banner, an appropriate picture, and great links with descriptions telling me where they'll take me and what they'll do for me work so much better than endless blocks of text, pictures, or sales-pitch. Keep it short, and make a regular user out of your first-time visitors.

15
WRITING PRODUCT DESCRIPTIONS

Sell, sell, sell. That's what product descriptions should do, sell your product. If your product descriptions aren't selling your product, you need to get new ones, and fast.

So what does it take to write a good website product description? And can writing a product description even really do anything to get a product sold? Let's take a look at what exactly goes into a great product description, and how they sell your product.

Target

Who are you selling to? It doesn't matter what you're selling, if you don't know who's buying, you've got problems. Of course your product by itself should give you a pretty good idea. If you're selling reading glasses, your target audience is people who have trouble seeing what their reading. If you're selling porn, your target audience is probably young men with too much time on their hands, and perhaps something else as well. Knowing who you're selling to, who you want to sell to, and who you can just forget about, is your first step in writing a website's product description.

Extol

Extol the virtues of your product. Shout them to the heavens. Let everyone and their dog know. If you don't list what's great about your product right from the get-go, why would anyone want to buy it? If your product is oatmeal, don't list the ingredients and where it was made first, tell me it will make my ass smaller! If toenail clippers are your specialty, don't tell me about the stainless steel metal right in the first line, tell me that yours don't make that annoying 'clipping' sound. Be up front with people about what you have, what it does, and how it can help them.

SEO

You've got to Search Engine Optimize (SEO) your product descriptions, no question about it. More than anything else on your site, people will be drawn to what you are selling; that's after all what you've got your website for, right? So you want to draw them into your products, and the best way to do that is by putting some SEO magic into each website product description. It's pretty easy to get all of your keywords into your product description, but just remember to not overdo it. You want a keyword density of about 1% to 2%, no more. Now, if you've got a 150 word product description, which many of them are, that means you can only put your keyword in there about 2 to 3 times. Anything else might be overkill, angering Google. If Google is angry, you'll lose traffic.

Show

Show people what your product can do for them, don't just tell them. Let them see your product description in their minds. If they're reading your text, they should be able to close their eyes and see what it is you're saying to them.

Her pants wouldn't stay up, and all of her belts were suddenly too big. What once took 30 minutes to squeeze into was now taking just seconds. And for the first time in years, she could see her toes. Now she starts every morning with Kiss Your Ass Goodbye Oatmeal, the brand that more overweight women everywhere are coming to call their own. So Kiss Your Ass Goodbye today, and have a lighter tomorrow!

16
WRITING REVIEW PAGES

People buy what other people buy. It might sound simple, but on the internet it's anything but.

Take Amazon.com. This internet retail giant does quite well for itself, and people who put their products up for sale on the site can also do quite well. That is if they have a few reviews to bolster their product's credentials.

Amazon is a great place to buy a book, and if you're one of the thousands of eBook authors out there today who are using Amazon to peddle your wares, you probably know this. But that's true only if people are buying your book. So what makes a complete stranger want to buy your book on Amazon? A good story, great characters, interesting places, and a decent price are all good selling points, but so are the reviews that you accumulate over time.

And that's the handle. It takes time after you've put a new product up on a website before it starts to get reviews. You may have sold 1,000 copies of your book, but perhaps you've only accumulated a few reviews, if any. And that's exactly the reason why people pay others to write reviews for their Amazon books, and other online products on a multitude of different websites.

Product reviews are great, and you should have some of them on your website. You can write them yourself, pay people to do it, or wait for others to do it honestly for you. After all, a review is supposed to come from someone who so loved your product that they're willing to take the time to go back to your website and write about it. And as mentioned before, this can take time, too much for some people.

Putting up 'fake' reviews could therefore be just the thing to get your products selling. Let's look at some ways you can dupe an unsuspecting public today.

Knowledge

If you're putting up a fake review, make sure that you or the person doing it for you is knowledgeable about the product they're talking about. You don't want someone saying that your new sun lotion is great at protecting against UV rays all day when it says "good for 2 hours" right in the product description above. On the other hand, you don't want someone coming across as too knowledgeable. If a person begins talking of how great and clean the sun lotion factory is, buyers will know that something fishy is going on.

Expertise

Reviews from experts are the best. If I'm buying sun lotion online and come across a review from a dermatologist, I'll be much more convinced about the product. Even if you can't find an expert to write a review for you, you can always find someone who's willing to do the research to sound like a doctor. And most people won't really care anyway if the person doing the review is speaking expertly about the subject.

Bogus Sun Lotion is great for a variety of reasons: It blocks both harmful UV and UVA rays from penetrating the outer dermal layer, while also protecting the thin cartilage membranes of the nose, an area prone to sunburns on most people.

It might not be from an expert, but who has to know?

Relevance

How can your product help me, and why should I buy it? Those are two of the top questions people will have when they're shopping around on the internet. A review that can answer both of those questions without sounding preachy or pathetically obvious is what you want on your site. If you're writing a review, make sure people know how the product helped you. You might also want to say why you chose that particular product over another possibly even cheaper product. And you want your review to make people think you'll buy it again, and in fact that's the only reason you're writing the review, because you were back on the site to make another purchase.

Let's look at what a great Bogus Sun Lotion review might look like:

Summer was upon us again, and my husband Mike and I were all set to get to the beach. The kids had been talking non-stop about going back again as soon as the weather turned hot, and I was a bit surprised. You see, all they could talk about last September was how they were never going to go to the beach again after the bad sunburns they all got on our last day. My husband and I never use cheap sun lotion, but the kind we bought must have been just that. I knew we should have gotten some online instead of from that beach kiosk. Even Mike and I got burned, and I think that's the first time for me since that girl's volleyball camp back in high school!

I began shopping around for cheap sun lotion online and came across Bogus Sun Lotion. It sounded good, and the price was certainly right, so I thought I'd give it a try. And am I glad I did! A few weeks ago Mike and I left the kids with his mother for the weekend and headed to a day spa. We both lounged around for quite a few hours in the sun, after using our Bogus Sun Lotion of course. Mike even fell asleep for an hour or so, but when we both woke up the next morning, all we had were great tans, and no burns. I can't wait to give the kids a great time at the beach this weekend, and you know I'll have my Bogus Sun Lotion close at hand.

This review is 267 words long, broken up into two block paragraphs, and has perfect spelling, grammar, and punctuation. It's also been SEO'd, meaning I've got my keywords in there to pull in more traffic. Did you notice them? They're "cheap sun lotion" and "Bogus Sun Lotion." Both have a keyword density of 1% - 2%, and with "sun lotion" in there as well as a main keyword, I'll probably get some hits for that. It has appears 5 times in the product review, and is pushing closer to 3% keyword density.

This is the type of review you want right at the top of your website's review pages. It has everything a site needs to pull someone in through SEO and then convince them to buy the product.

17
WRITING AN IN THE NEWS PAGE

Websites need to constantly change. They have to evolve, get better, and offer something new. If someone goes to your website, likes it a lot, forgets about it, and comes back a year later, what will they see? New and exciting content, better pictures, more downloads, and a whole lot to tell their friends about? Or the exact same thing they saw last year?

Hopefully your website looks and sounds like the former, and not the latter. But how do you make people realize what's new about your site, without them having to dig through all of your website's pages in the process? You add a new page called "In the News," that's how.

I've written several In the News website pages for people, and they're nearly all the same. People want to tell other people what newspapers and other publications have mentioned their website, as well as inform general users what new features the site has. There are many ways you can go about writing an In the News page, and here are a few tips to get you started.

The Media

The best thing to put on your In the News page is any mentions your website may have gotten from the media. This doesn't have to be the national news, or even a large regional paper. Simple write-ups in your local newspaper, a mention on the local news, or even an advertisement in a magazine are all newsworthy; it's why they're on the news, after all!

Any publicity is good publicity, so take advantage of it and list it on your In the News page. Remember, people who are new to your site or just haven't been there in quite some time won't know much about the local media in your area, so why not give them a head's up?

Highlight Changes

Lots of people think that they can't talk about anything that's newsworthy when it comes to their site, but this simply isn't true. Make sure you highlight what's old in a new way. Have you added a new product or great series of articles recently? How about some new downloads, even if they're just a few simple pictures? And don't be afraid to mention your traffic. If you've got nothing else to write about, consider telling everyone that you just passed 10,000 users this month, or even 100. It might not make headlines around the world, but it will give you something to talk about, and content for you In the News page.

Old is New

You're putting articles up on your site, right? Good. Now why not add a new page and bunch many similar topics together. For instance, if you really got into green Jell-O a few months ago and wrote about it for a week straight, why not bunch all of your Jell-O articles together so that anyone searching for your fixation won't have to click around a lot. And what about your products? Have those product descriptions just been sitting there collecting electronic dust for the past 6 months or so? Why not spice them up a bit, adding a paragraph here or there. It doesn't have to be revolutionary or earth-shattering, but it can be listed on your In the News page.

18
WRITING A FOOTER

There are lots of things that go into writing a website, so let's start at the bottom, since it's so much simpler than the top.

Few people surfing the internet will ever make it to the bottom of your page, except for a cursory scroll to see how long the page actually is. Everyone knows that the meat-and-potatoes of any website are at the top, or close to it, so that leaves all the boring but necessary stuff for the bottom.

But does it have to be boring? I don't think so, and that's why I routinely head to the bottom of most websites I visit. Here are some of the things I see, and find quite useful:

Copyright

Putting your copyright is a good first step, and one of the reasons you should create a Footer right away. Tell the world that this content is yours, and you're willing to fight for it.

Back to Top

Also consider a button that will shoot the user right back up to the top of the page. This is especially handy when you've got a super long page that will take a lot of scrolling to get through.

Links

Give your user all of the great options listed at the top of your page, but now in simple text format with links. Save the flashy stuff for the top of your page; put the basic infrastructure at the bottom. When I'm shooting around the internet doing work, I'll often go right to the bottom of the page if I want to contact someone, learn more about the site, or just find the simple directional links that I know will be harder to find with all the content taking up space at the top of the page.

Address

Go ahead and put your physical contact information down there in the Footer as well, if you've still got space. Letting people know where you are in the world is a great idea for building trust, and you can even put in a cool link to a map that will pinpoint the exact spot. No one may ever use it, but hey, it shows you mean business. And if you're thinking about, or already have a Contact page, make sure you link to it in your Footer.

Language

Language selectors are a great option if you have a particularly large e-commerce site that's pulling in traffic from all over the world. Letting someone choose Chinese when that's their native language will go a long way in making them feel comfortable on your site, and coming back in the future.

About Us

About us blurbs are another wonderful option for your Footer. I've seen many authors put a small photo and a short bio of themselves at the bottom of certain articles or other content pages. It's always nice to see a picture of the person who's supposedly doing the writing.

News/Awards

News organizations that have highlighted your website, or even given it an award, should be one of the first things you put in your Footer. While you probably already have these on your In The News page, there's no reason not to tell people again, or those like me who always rush to the bottom of the page first and ignore the rest of your site.

Posts

Recent posts that you've noticed getting a lot of traffic might be a good candidate for your Footer. It's not always easy getting to past blog posts or articles when you're adding new ones each day, and an article directory somewhere else on your site might not be doing as good of a job as it could. If you have a sitemap page on your website, it'll serve the same function, so link to it.

With all of the great tips above, you should now have a massive Footer that takes up half of your page. That's not a very good option. It's a Footer after all, not a 'knee-er' or 'legger,' and certainly not an 'armer' or 'upper bodier,' whatever that is.

Keep the Footer small, but keep your ideas for it big. If you run your website right and keep it fresh and relevant, you'll soon have lots of options for your Footer, perhaps even too many. More and more I'm seeing Footers that have ten links, graphics for awards, and media affiliate logos. This causes the Footer to take up nearly a whole screen. Big e-commerce sites are doing it, and perhaps it's the latest thing, but I've always found it a bit unsettling. If you've made it this for in the book you know I'm all about being short and concise with your content.

One final note: there is no chapter on Headers. If you want a header, just put some links in it, a shopping cart, and very little else. The top of your page is your Header.

19
WRITING A SITE MAP

Site Maps are complicated. Not everyone wants to mess around with making one, submitting it to search engines, and getting it all worked out and configured correctly on their site. If you're selling products, however, a Site Map could be a very useful and perhaps even necessary thing.

People are looking for things to buy each and everyday. They do product searches in Google simply by typing the name of whatever they're looking for into Search. It doesn't matter what you type in, anything from aardvark hair to zebra costumes will come up. And you can buy them.

So why are they coming up in Search? Probably for a few reasons, including Search Engine Optimized (SEO) content, lots of visitors, and a Site Map. You see, if you make a Site Map and submit it to the big search engines like Google, Yahoo, and Bing, you'll get those products indexed and listed when someone searches them. That might not put you up on page one of the SERP, but you'll be well on your way.

Google is the real expert on Site Maps, and they'll give you just about all the information you could want. It's not the easiest to read, however. Here are some of the main points that Google makes:

Great Content

You've got to have great content for Google to be interested in you. They have millions of websites going through their Search results each day, and unless you've got something new, or just better, they're not that interested.

But Google can't always find that great content by itself. That's why a Site Map is important. A Site Map lists all of your links, from one page to another, and it tells Google what they are and how they interact. This makes it easier to find your site and index it. That makes it easier for you to get to the top of Google.

Difficult Finds

When you start to make an e-commerce site, you'll quickly find that it grows and grows. What started out as a few pages quickly becomes dozens, and then hundreds depending on how many products you've got. If each one of those products has its own page, it could be difficult for users, you, and Google to navigate.

That's when Site Maps really come in handy. If you can take the time to sit down and thoroughly go through your site, you'll benefit in the long-term. Copy and paste all of those URLs into a document that you can access easily. That will form the basis of your Site Map. As soon as you've got all of your URLs on one page, or dozens as often happens, you'll really get an idea of what your site looks like when its been stripped down to the bones.

That's what Google likes to see, and if you can clean that up and edit it to their standards, they'll be quite happy when you submit it. And if you're submitting your site to Google, that means you won't have to wait for the googlebot to crawl by and index your site. That could save you time, and create more visitors and customers for you sooner.

Indexing Images

Search engines don't count images as content. They can't easily scan them to see what they are, that would just take too long. You're already impatient having to wait months for the googlebot to crawl through millions of pages before it gets to you, how about waiting a few years?

If you list your images in your Site Map, search engines like Google will know about them. And perhaps more importantly, users that want to search your site by using the Site Map will know about them. When I go to a really large site, I'll sometimes pull up the Site Map. It's usually right at the bottom of the page, with a clear link to it. That makes it easier for me to search through all of their links to see exactly what I'm looking for.

Lots of users like your content and your images, but they don't always want to see them when they're looking for something fast. A Site Map will solve that problem for them by directing them to exactly what they're looking for.

Limited Links

You'll have two main problems when it comes to your links, and a Site Map can help you with both. First, you may not be getting any incoming links. No one else out there on the internet is linking to you. That makes it hard for Google to find your site, and it takes longer as a result. When you have more links pointing to you, Google will notice them on other sites and index them. This will get you noticed, and that will help your rankings.

There are a few things you can do to get those incoming links. First, write great content, that's a given. But it's not always enough to get you those links quickly. That's when a bit more footwork comes in. You've got to go to sites similar to yours, perhaps with a blog, and make your presence known.

This could be anything from sending an email saying what you offer that could help that site, to leaving a blog comment. Consider finding relevant forums to your site, and posting in them as well. For that to be effective, you've got to do it each week, and write quality posts. If you just write quick promos, people will think it's spam, and it'll probably cost you users.

The other side of the coin is your own internal links. If you've got a large site, it might be difficult for Google to understand what is going on. That's why you need clear links from one page to the next.

Link all of your product description pages to your shopping cart or checkout pages. Don't have stray links that lead nowhere, or to sites that have nothing to do with you. If you've taken a product or page down, make sure you find and remove all links to it. Check and make sure all of your blog comments are indexed properly, especially if you're showing them in a 'recent posts' sidebar. The clearer things are to you, your users, and to Google, the better your site will get ranked.

Backdoor Blues

When someone finds your site using Search, they'll often find one of your back pages. Some kind of keyword you had on a certain page drew them to that page, and not your home page. They may not be exactly sure how your site works, so you've got to tell them. These people are like those that arrive at a party unannounced and with no friends. They'll feel wary at first, and may want to leave. You've got to be a good host, walk up and put your arm around them and invite them inside.

That's what your Site Map is, a welcoming host. It's a list of links that tell people and search engines what is on your site. Make sure you've got a short and clear description for each of those links. This will make it easy for users to see what they'll be going to. It'll also make Google happy because it won't think your site is just a link farm. Link farms are just endless pages of links that a lot of black-hat SEO-types like to use to try and drive traffic up to their sites. They'll attract people with useless links, but by then they've gotten another visitor. Google penalizes them heavily now.

You won't have to worry about these shady practices because you won't be doing them. By putting that clear description down, everyone benefits, and especially you. If you don't label your links, you might even forget what each of them is exactly.

Play around with making a Site Map. Go to other sites and check out theirs, and also search out other information. You've got to know about computer jargon to get one finished, but when you do it'll be well worth it.

20
WRITING A TERMS OF USE

A Terms of Use is boring. There's no other way to put it. No one really wants to read them, and you certainly don't want to write one. But having one on your e-commerce site is critical if you've got a lot of customers. It doesn't matter if your selling services, digital products, or physical products, having a Terms of Use is important. It will protect you from lawsuits, and it will often work in your favor when a dispute arises.

So how do you write a Terms of Use? Very carefully, that's how. Most people hire a lawyer to write a Terms of Use for them, and this is the best idea. You're working with legal concepts, issues of liability, and copyrights, as well as who'll be left holding the bag when things go south. Do yourself a favor if you've got a large e-commerce site that has lots of customers, and get yourself a lawyer.

If you don't want to, well, I'll tell you how I've written Terms of Use documents for other people. I've worked with websites wanting to put them up, and I've worked with people putting stuff in the iStore for iPhone Apps.

What I did on both occasions was to go to sites similar to those sites and look at what they had. I'd read their Terms of Use, and copied it. That's right, I'd copy it right into Word and begin working on it. By the time I was done it was not the same and not a copy; it was a new Terms of Use because the language was different, but the meaning and legal jargon was still the same.

Let's say that you've got a great new product that is similar to what's already selling in the iStore. Go to those sites and see what they have. Get their Terms of Use, copy it, and take out all reference to that company. You can do this with a simple Find/Replace in MS Word. After that, you've got to find the parent company of that company. That's right; many large companies are affiliated with others. Those parent companies will be listed in the Terms of Use, and you don't want any mention of them.

When you write a Terms of Use, you'll have several major sections. It's best to tackle each one of these one at a time. Your finished Terms of Use will be around 5,000 words long and it'll take up a good 12 to 15 pages in MS Word depending on your formatting. You don't want that appearing all as one block of text, so you've got to break it up. Here are a few headings that you want to include:

- Basic Terms;
- General Conditions;
- Rules Regarding Content;
- Medical & Legal Questions;
- Limitation of Liability, Waiver;
- Miscellaneous.

Those are the sections, with some minor variations, that you'll see in other Terms of Use documents you seek out. Just listing them gives me a headache, and we haven't even gotten into what each of them means, and what they should say. Let's go through them each individually.

Basic Terms

These will be listed in a numbered format, usually from 1 to 15 or 20. They'll lay down common things, such as age restrictions, sexual content restrictions, how a user is responsible for their own account, login information for you and other users, community guidelines for forums or blogs, issues of illegality, spam, interactions with other users, and violations of the terms.

Each of those points will get its own numbered paragraph. Some will be longer than others, with your account and how you use it taking up the most space. You can get a good feel for what this looks like when you find a Terms of Use on one of the sites you are a member of or use regularly.

General Conditions

This section will also be numbered with each condition appearing in a small block format. This is where you as a website and as a retailer tell the user that the conditions of the Terms of Use could change at anytime. You have the power to suspend service to your users, and you can change how things are bought, sold, or posted on your website. When you lay these out clearly and up front, it makes it obvious that you have the final say in matters, and you limit your legal liability.

Rules Regarding Content

This section will often be included with sites that allow content to be posted onto them. So if you've got a blog that lots of people are posting to, this is a good section to include. It details how all materials posted have to abide by copyrights of others. You don't want someone posting the newest bestselling novel on your site, and you want to limit your legal liability if that does happen. If a user were to do something like that, and the book's author or publisher found out, you'll have eliminated most problems. The user had to accept your Terms of Use as one of the stipulations of putting up content, and this is a clear violation of that. You'll be in the clear if you can get this into your Terms of Use.

This also eliminates any liability that you'll incur when someone else complains about that content. Say that someone put up some sexually explicit images on your site. Now image that an 8-year old kid saw those and went complaining to mom. She could take action against you. If you've made it clear that you prohibit this, but also that you can't prevent all of that content from appearing all of the time, you've limited your liability. If you've got a forum with thousands of people posting each day, some things are bound to fall through the cracks. You need to put this into your Rules Regarding Content section.

Medical & Legal Questions

If your site offers health products, has a blog that gives health advice, or offers any kind of service that is in any way related to health, you'll want this section. Medical & Legal Questions is a section that is usually bulleted. You can start to tell that each section has its own special formatting considerations, which makes the Terms of Use easy to wade through.

In this section you want to make it clear that the advice being offered on your blog and forum posts is not that of a medical professional. Well, what if you are a medical professional? I'd still put it in your Terms of Use, because you can't be a professional on everything. Doctors that know about the heart might not know that much about skin ailments, for instance.

Make it clear in this section that doctors should be consulted if a user has a serious medical condition. The advice offered is not meant to replace that offered by a professional. Also say something to the effect of getting to a hospital right away if you're feeling ill. You don't want someone suing you a few months down the road because they were waiting for your next blog post when they should have been going to the ER.

Limitation of Liability, Waiver

This section is in all caps. IT WILL LOOK LIKE THIS. Yes, the whole section would appear that someone is yelling. Either that makes it the most important section of your Terms of Use, or just the most difficult to read. Keep with the all caps because that's what everyone else does. I don't know why, you'll have to consult a lawyer.

The first block will be short, and say something to the effect that you will under no circumstances be liable. This could be you, your website, or your company. Make sure you put the names in there.

The next section is much larger, and each sentence starts with a letter. A) So each sentence will look something like this. B) The next sentence will look like this.

You'll continue like that until about letter 'H.' This is one of the most difficult sections of your Terms of Use to write. You can't change much of the language because it's very specific. You'll just have to do the best you can to copy some other site's and try your best to change it. Remember, you're saying in your Terms of Use that you respect copyrights. That means that your Terms of Use can't be a copy. But that doesn't mean you can't learn from others, and change things around just enough to make it unique. Still, if you're a large site, get a lawyer.

The final section will talk about damages, injunctions, and how a user may be waiving some of their rights by using your service or products. You'll also not be responsible for what other users do. A lot of this has been talked about in other sections, and I get the strong impression that the Liability section is just a way to reinforce everything that's been said earlier.

The next section will be called Indemnification, and it will be separated.

Indemnification: You'll write it just like this, with all of your text coming out from that main word. What this lays out is how a user will have to hold you harmless for anything they think they could complain about. You'll have about 2 to 3 sentences saying this in legal jargon, and then smaller sections set off with lowercase Roman numerals. (i) Each of those sections will really just be one sentence. (ii) They'll all follow this format. (iii) In this section you'll again go over how you can't be held liable. (iv) Look at how other Terms of Use do this, and you'll have a good idea.

The next section is called Copyright Violations, and it will look like this:

COPYRIGHT VIOLATIONS. It will tell your user that you have a lot of respect for copyrights, and that you'll not allow copyrighted material to be infringed upon. In this section you ask users to point out content on your site that may be copyrighted, and you'll ask them to contact you. All of the points under this section will be numbered. So you'll have one number asking for their user information, another for the content in question, and another for their address, phone number, and the like. You'll probably have about 6 numbers here.

Miscellaneous

You probably didn't think there could be anymore, did you? Well, we're almost through. The Miscellaneous section will only be about two large paragraphs, and it will try to tie up any of those loose ends that may not have fit into any of the other categories.

This section again lays out the rights you have in regard to complaints and liability, but it's a lot less legal sounding. This would be the spot to write out some specifics about your site in a way that is easier to read and understand for you. You should have gotten most of the main points covered by now, so this is where you sum them up.

After that you're done. Go back and make sure the formatting looks good. Compare it to other Terms of Use documents that are out there. Make sure nothing is too similar. All Terms of Use are similar, but you don't want yours to be blatantly obvious. This is mainly for when disputes arise, which hopefully they never will. Most users will accept this right away without reading it if you have that as a condition of their user account. If you don't, even fewer will read it. But it's there if the need arises, giving you some peace of mind.

21
WRITING A PRIVACY POLICY

You'll often see Privacy Policies on large social networking sites. These tell users what is expected of them. It tells them what good content is, and that they should refrain from adding bad content. They're usually in the context of blog comments or forum posts.

A Privacy Policy is different from a Terms of Use. Terms of Use are legally binding documents that can be produced in court. They're often written by a lawyer. They say what a user can and can't do, and are pretty much the rules of the site.

A Privacy Policy just tells the user what will happen with the contact information they supply to a website. So if you're collecting a lot of emails, names, and other personal information from your users, you'll probably need a Privacy Policy.

You'll collect a lot of information from the users of your site involuntarily. User information is collected from cookies each time they visit. Cookies uniquely identify you to a site so that they can recognize what your computer system is.

More and more people are using mobile devices to access the internet, and cookies will tell this to a site. You'll also be able to get those personalized advertisements that seem to follow you around the web. Checkout information can also be stored with cookies. Cookies will be essential to your site if you're involved in e-commerce. They allow your user to go to the shopping cart and checkout. While it's true that many users can turn cookies off, or even be notified each time a site wants to add one, most choose to just accept them automatically.

Many times you'll ask your users for information directly. This can be through an email newsletter, a contact form, and of course financial information. Whenever someone provides a review of one of your products they'll often be asked to provide information. Someone that creates a user account for a forum, or supplies contact information to make a blog post, will also provide information to you. And of course there's the big one that most people want, the information you get when someone makes a purchase.

So what do you do with all that contact information that you have about people? Do you share it with other sites? Do you sell it to other sites that will often pay good money for such juicy contacts? Or do you use it to make your site better, or just nothing at all?

Those are the questions you'll need to answer in your Privacy Policy. Here are few pointers on getting started:

Identify

Identifying what information you collect from your user should be the first thing you do when you write your Privacy Policy. Explain that you get their information from contact forms, email signups, and newsletters. Tell them how cookies may learn about them and which pages and products they click on. Talk about any information that may be collected if someone is accessing your site from a mobile device. And explain that with each email sent, contact information is exchanged.

Explain

The next thing to do is to explain what you do with that information. If you're selling it to other sites, tell your user that here. I'd bet that many of your users might not like that if they were to read it, however. I would state flat out that you don't sell information because you value your visitors and customers.

After that explain how the information you do have is shared. This could be through affiliates or other businesses working with you; third-party service providers like those involved in shipping a product; when legal questions come into play and law enforcement asks for that information; and when the user asks for it to be shared.

Allow

Allow users to opt out of your Privacy Policy. Lots of people are mistrustful of new sites that they don' t know. Perhaps they've been scammed before or had their contact information taken advantage of. It's real easy for a stray social security number to ruin someone's bank account or tax return, and you don't want to be the cause of that.

Explain to users that they can opt out of certain features and services on your site that request information. These can be things like the checkout process, which means they probably won't be buying anything. It can also be the cookies that they can disable, as many people won't know about that. Some users accidentally get on an email list, and you can tell them how they can get off of it. And if users can adjust their own preferences on your site, explain how they can do that or put a link to where it is. Oftentimes you can let the user adjust their own accounts as necessary if you've got a particularly large e-commerce site.

Ease

Ease people's fears with your Privacy Policy. Tell them how secure your site is, and how their financial and contact information is protected. If you're using advanced software to protect your site and the users, tell them. Explain that only the last 4-digits of a social security number will be listed. Tell them that only the last digits of a bank account will be listed. And explain how important it is for users to keep their passwords safe. You can only go so far in protecting people, so let them know they have a part to play as well.

There are many great sites out there on the internet that will provide Privacy Policy templates, generators, or just simple advice. You'll also learn a lot by just browsing around some Privacy Policies that are out there. Go to Google and Amazon and look at theirs. Check out those on your favorite online newspapers. And see how the companies whose products fill your home do their Privacy Policies.

You'll learn more than enough to write your site's Privacy Policy simply, and effectively. Remember, most people aren't going to look at this. But it's there if they want to, though that doesn't mean it has to be long and arduous. Write a short Privacy Policy letting your user know you care about them and that you won't do anything to hurt them. It's pretty much that simple.

This is what the Privacy Policy on one of my own websites looks like:

BigSkyWords Privacy Policy

I value you as a visitor and user of my site. I want you to know which contact information is collected from you when you visit bigskywords.com and what is done with that information.

First, let me say that no one other than myself, Greg Strandberg, is using your contact information, or even receiving it. All of that is private and not going anywhere.

The information that this site collects does so in the following ways:

> **Cookies**: Each time you visit a cookie may be created. Additional cookies might be created when you go to new pages on the site. If you'd like to disable these cookies or have them tell you when a request is made, you can do that on your browser.
>
> **Email List**: If you choose to sign up for the bigskywords.com email list, you're giving me your contact information. This will consist of your first name, email address, and username. I'll add that to the list which tells user when a new blog post is added.
>
> **Contact Form**: When you use the contact form, you'll be providing your first name, email address, and username. I'll read this and get back to you if you've asked a question. This information will not be shared or posted on the site.
>
> **Blog Posts**: If you choose to comment on one of the blog posts, you will be supplying contact information about yourself. Your blog posts are your responsibility, and any personal information you supply in them is done voluntarily.

22
WRITING A CONTACT PAGE

If you want your website to be trusted, you've got to put a Contact page on it. This is one of the easiest pages on your website to write, but there are still a few points you want to follow.

First, keep it short. You should have explained who you are in your About Us page. All you need to do on your Contact page is tell your visitors and users where you are in the world and how you can be reached. Second, give them an easy way to contact you. A simple email link or contact form is more than sufficient for anything online, and one phone number will do fine.

There are several things you should list on your website's Contact page.

Physical Address

Always put down your mailing address. While it may be true that you're only doing business on the internet, the fact that you don't seem to exist in the real world is enough to give some people pause. It's not difficult to list your mailing address, and chances are no one will ever use it. But it does give a certain peace of mind to users who see it there. And it gives you an added level of legitimacy.

Phone

Put down the phone numbers that are associated with your business. If this is the office phone for your website's headquarters, great! If it's your home phone, well, throw that up too. Chances are if you're small no one is going to call it, and it won't generate a lot of junk phone calls. Instead it adds just another level of expertise and relevance to your site.

Email

This seems like a no-brainer, but if you're not using a regularly-checked email address, you could be setting yourself up for problems. You might have a separate personal and website email, and if that's the case you need to check your website's email account on a daily basis, and most likely more. Large e-commerce sites will need full-time staffs just to handle the email volume, so this could be an area of concern.

Finally, consider how your email appears to your visitor or user. Does it pop them out to Microsoft Outlook? I don't use that, I hate it when that program pops up on me, and I'm surely not alone. Many users like to copy the address into their Hotmail or Gmail account directly and send from there. List your email twice: once in plain text, and another time as a link. That way you'll make everyone happy.

Directions

Telling someone how to get to your physical location is great, and you might even want to include a photo and a link to Google Maps. The Contact page is great chance for websites catering mainly to local markets to show themselves off. Auto repair shops do particularly well with Contact pages that act as a second About Us page.

Just make sure you're not missing out on the most important function of your Contact page, which is getting contacted. Always put your contact submission form near the top of your page, and make sure it's not cluttered by other content that could lead to user distractions.

This is what my own website has as its Contact page:

Contact

Please feel free to drop BigSkyWords a line on anything about Montana, writing, or writing work you'd like done.

BigSkyWords Mailing Address
Wang hai hui jing yuan Building B #1604

Shekou, Nanshan District, Shenzhen,
Guangdong Province, China 518067
中国广东省深圳市南山区蛇口望海汇景苑 B 楼 1604
518067

Phone: +086 15019496367

Wikipedia Page on Shenzhen:
http://en.wikipedia.org/wiki/Shenzhen

Your mail, emails, and phone calls will not be shared with anyone. Feel free to use the email form for quick and easy communication. And don't be afraid to tell me what you like and don't like about BigSkyWords. I'm always trying to make the site better, and your voice counts!

This was a really old contact page I had when I was living in China. It worked quite well, and lots of people may have been a bit more interested in me and my site because of what was on that page.

23
WRITING A FAQ

No matter how good you make your website, how simply you write the content, or how easy you make it to contact you, people will have questions. You could put a big flashing banner on your site explaining a certain product's price, and you'd still get questions about it.

That's why creating a Frequently Asked Questions (FAQ) page is so important for expanding e-commerce websites, websites that are large and have many uses or functions, and those that just want to challenge the competition.

It's a simple way to interact with your new visitors and regular users, and it really saves you time. If your website's growing, you've probably noticed the uptick in emails and possibly even phone calls. Many of those questions and concerns you're getting could easily be dealt with in a simple FAQ.

Having a FAQ also imparts trust to your users. By putting a FAQ up on your website, you're showing your user that you'll do everything possible to answer their questions and make their time on your site as enjoyable and easy as possible. You're not only saving yourself time, but you're saving your user time.

Scrolling through a FAQ tells users that you take the time to thoughtfully answer their questions and that you have a big enough site to warrant a lot of questions in the first place. Both will create more credibility for your website in their eyes, and will go a long way in turning that visitor into a user.

Let's look at a few ways you can write your FAQ or make your existing FAQ better:

Be Direct

When people want answers, they don't want a lot of beating around the bush. They're looking for an authoritative answer, so give it to them. Don't sugarcoat and don't dilly-dally. Just tell them straight-up.

Remember, if your FAQ is poorly written or poorly presented, it could do more harm than good. Additionally, don't use your FAQ to sell your products. You have product pages and descriptions for that. Doing that will only create mistrust in your user's eyes, and cause you to lose credibility.

Be Simple

If your site is selling knives, don't go into how stainless steel is made. Just tell them the steel's name and measurements. People aren't looking for the answers to the questions of the universe, either. Keep things simple, and to the point. And make them simple to see. Formatting your FAQ in clear Q&A bullets under simple headings is a proven approach that works for people.

Be Concise

Say what you want to say in 2 to 3 lines or less. If you force yourself to make your answer short, it will force you to make it clearer. If the question is extremely difficult, make the answer even shorter.

Be Organized

Have an outline of how your questions and answers are going to be organized. Create categories for each of them, such as products, payments, and account. Make sure each section is clearly separated from the others.

Also, put your simplest questions at the top of your FAQ and your more difficult questions toward the bottom. Many people can find exactly what they're looking for by glancing at the first few questions, saving them time and hassle.

Be Easy

It's not always easy admitting you need help, and users that go to your FAQ are doing just that. They need help with a question, so give them an easy answer. Go easy on them too; no one wants to be browbeaten or made to feel the fool.

Make your FAQ easy to navigate. If you've got a lot of questions and answers, put up a hyperlinked list or table of contents at the top of the page. Don't forget those 'return to the top' links either. Getting someone to the top of your FAQ should be just as easy as getting them to the bottom.

Be There

Don't hide your FAQ. Put it right down in your footer or even up in your header. Make the link clear, and make sure it works. You might not get a lot of visitors to your FAQ page, but at least it will be there for anyone who wants it.

Being there also means making changes. You'll still get emails and phone calls if you're a large site, and some of those questions and concerns may be things you've not yet addressed in your FAQ. Make a list of these each week and schedule time to update your FAQ accordingly.

24
WRITING SEO

Let's take a look at the acronym 'SEO.' You see this thrown around a lot these days, especially if you're writing on the internet. "Everyone wants SEO, everyone needs SEO, if your website doesn't have SEO, you might as well be dead." Those are common sentiments, and they have some validity.

But SEO is not the do or die thing that many people make it out to be. It is, however, important to your website, and you should at least learn the basics. SEO stands for Search Engine Optimization. Let's take a look at each one of those words individually.

Search

I've seen figures that say up to 92% of people on the internet use search engines to find information. How they do that is by typing in a word, phrase, or short sentence into a search engine. By far the most popular search engine is Google.

When you type your 'keyword' into Google, it will display the Search Engine Result Pages, or SERP. This is the list that comes up, usually with 10 pages on it. Those are the hottest, most popular, and what Google thinks to be the best pages for what you typed in.

Most people will click on that first result, or perhaps even the first two or three. Rarely will people begin looking at the next 10 results, and if you're coming up on page 4 or later, you're probably not going to be seen at all.

This is why SEO is so important for Search. You've got to have the keyword that people are typing into Google on your website if you want to come up on the top of Google's SERP.

Consider the classic 1980s film *The Princess Bride*. In the film the character Inigo Montoya has a familiar catchphrase or keyword. Each time he sees someone he tells them he's looking for the "six-fingered man." He's constantly searching for that man, or keyword if you will, and the more he says it, the more it becomes known. Everyone knows if they want to find out anything about the 'six-fingered man,' all they've got to do is ask Inigo Montoya.

You want your website to be like Inigo Montoya and his "six-fingered man." If you can use your keyword enough times, just like in *The Princess Bride*, you'll eventually come up on top. How often should you have that keyword on your website? You need a ratio of 1% to 2% on each page where that keyword is the top keyword. This will help you when people use Search. And if you don't believe me, just type in "six-fingered man" into Google and see what comes up.

Engine

An engine is a machine. It can run all day and run all night, so long as you keep fueling it. Man made engines to make his life easier, but they may have only made it more difficult.

When it comes to the Engine in SEO, we're talking about Google again. But we're also talking about what Google can do. These Engines of the web are quite the workers. They scour the internet day and night for new and fresh content. They do this because they want to make a complete index of the internet. That's millions and perhaps billions of pages. That takes time, and if one of these engines has indexed your site, chances are it won't be back again anytime soon unless it detects some new content.

And remember, these engines are unfeeling machines. To quote one of my favorite lines from the 1980s film *Short Circuit*, "They don't get happy, they don't get sad, they just run programs." These programs that they're running enable them to look at your content, look at your pages, and determine if your website is good or not. If you check-out, they'll bump you up in their rankings. If you don't, you'll get dinged and go down.

They'll also look at your retention rate. How long are your visitors staying on your pages? Are people coming and going faster than at that meth house down the street? This kind of revolving door, or bounce rate, on your website won't help you, and will in fact hurt you.

Think about all the times you go to a site that you didn't want to, or that you quickly found out was rubbish? What did you do? You hit 'back' faster than a man on a one-way street hits the brakes. That tells Google that the site in question is not good, the bad neighborhood kid, and one that others should stay away from. Don't let that be you.

Optimization

One of my favorite movies from the 1980s was *Mannequin*. Boy was it cheesy! But I started thinking about it in relation to Optimization one day. You see, in the movie they were constantly changing up the window dressing of the window display. They wanted to make those mannequins look as good as they could, but also the things surrounding them. It created this great look that caused people walking by on the street to stop and stare, and perhaps more importantly for the department store, start talking.

You want your website's Optimization to be just like that window display in *Mannequin*. Get those people that otherwise would have passed you by to stop and look. Remember, the longer someone stays on your pages, the better you'll be in the eyes of Google. So to Optimize, you need to make everything on that page better. Your content has to be great, it has to look great, and your website has to function great. You need to give people value. And you need to play on their emotions.

Those people surfing on the internet are just like those walking by on the street. They're looking for something catchy to grab their eye, and if they see it on your site, they'll stop, look, and talk. They might even go inside and buy something, even if it wasn't what was in that window.

Optimization is organization. You're organized, things are done, everything looks good, and now you can rest. When your site is as good as it can be, you'll have great Optimization. And that's often the same thing as great content.

25
WRITING CRO

A great way to start targeting your audience is through Conversion Rate Optimization (CRO). This is how many of the visitors to your site become the customers of your site. Whether you're trying to increase your sales or just your blog readers, CRO is a necessary tool in your bag, and one that isn't all that difficult.

If you've got 10,000 people going to your site each day, that's great. But if you've only got a conversion rate of 1%, you'll get frustrated fast and wonder why everyone is shopping, but no one is buying. There are two important terms to think about in relation to CRO: bounce rate and click-through-rate.

Bounce rate is when a user sees one page, and then goes away. If you have a bounce rate of 20% then 20% of your visitors see your page and take a bounce. That's a really low number, and most sites will have a higher rate. Getting a number like 20% requires a lot of perfecting of the pages that are getting a lot of hits. If you can impress someone who found your site through a search engine, they might click-through to your site.

The click-through-rate is how many people are actually coming to your site from a third party. This third party could be another site that's linked to you, some kind of email with your site's information, or an advertisement. If you're running paid ads that are placed on search engines or other sites, you'll often get hits to your page as a result.

These are your most important visitors to convert to customers. They've already been enticed by what they saw in your ad, now you have to keep them interested. If you've got a good landing page that allows them to go right to the product they're interested in, you'll have a good level of CRO.

The bounce rate needs to be addressed if you want to keep your online sales growing. The click-through-rate needs to be increased if it's working, or the advertising campaign tweaked if it's not. You need to make your website shine and stand out from all the others out there. Convince people that they need your product, not just want it. Let them know that they can trust you, and the products that you're selling.

One of the best ways to decrease your bounce rate is to have good content that helps your user. There are a few simple and easy ways to get started with lowering that number, and implementing your site with CRO.

Testing

When you finally get around to publishing that website, you're feeling pretty good. Everything looks good, and everything seems to work. But does it? You're rather biased, after all. When it comes to making a website, it's real easy to miss a few things. You might have even gone over something so many times that the mistakes just seem natural, which of course makes them impossible to see.

That's why they have lots of great testing websites that will go through your site and tell you exactly what they liked and what they didn't like, and how you can change or improve this to get more buyers.

Sites like usabilla.com and fivesectiontest.com will analyze your site for free, and paid sites like usertesting.com will do so for a nominal fee. You can also get software that will do the same thing, such as Tealeaf and Clicktale.

If you don't know what you're doing wrong, how can you know what to do right? These sites will present unbiased views, mainly because you've already paid them. They'll charge you quite a bit depending on the size of your site, but that could be an investment that really pays dividends in the future.

If you'd like to find a cheaper approach, consider many of the freelance websites that are out there. Sites like guru.com, fiverr.com, and freelancer.com will all have people that design websites for others, and who will take a look at yours. Most will point out what you need to do to increase your CRO, and most will help you do it.

You might end up paying a fraction of the cost of some of the more established internet brands if you outsource to someone in India or Bangladesh. Still, quality is what you want, and you often get what you pay for. If you're building a site in the evenings after work, this approach will probably work great for you. If you're an established company that wants measurable results quickly, it might be better to stick to the CRO experts.

Helping

The internet empowers us. We can speak our mind, go where we want, and buy things that we'd never consider in a regular store. That creates a sense of independence in users, and they're proud of their ability to find their own deals, and their own answers. If you can give them something to go off of to solve their problems, such as a FAQ, user guide, or even a public messaging platform or service, they'll appreciate your site, and potentially buy something.

How many times have you gone to a large online retailer like Amazon or eBay? Those sites are huge, with millions of products. Wading through them to find exactly what it is you're looking for can be difficult. Running into problems happens quiet frequently, and it's often not the easiest thing to find answers.

Don't let your users feel overwhelmed by your site. Give them user guides and help sections that are clear, easy to read, and to the point. Make the links to them clearly visible on your pages, like right at the top. People who need help and get it will feel much more comfortable when it comes to giving you their money.

Analyzing

Use Google Analytics and Adsense. These tools will tell you how many people are coming to your site, and where they're coming from. When people get directed to your site from another site, you'll know. Go to that site and check them out. See what they have, and how it's similar to what you have.

Why did your user come to you from them? Was it because that site didn't have what they were looking for? Was the price too high? The user interface and checkout system bad? Or could it be that there is a link to your site on that site?

These are all great questions to ask yourself when you're looking at the sites leading to you. You can learn a lot from this type of research, and setting aside a little time each day or week to do this will benefit you in the long-term.

That research will come in real handy when it comes to designing your pages. You can take what you think is working from your competitors and make it better. Put it up on your site in a new and unique way that interests that user who came from them to you. By doing that you've got a much better chance of turning that user into a customer.

Presenting

How do you present your content, and yourself? Mainly through the words and images you display on your website's pages. More and more however, people are putting up videos on their sites to show themselves and their products. This can be a great tool for turning a visitor into a customer, and if you're in some fields, it's almost a must.

Consider the medical and health field. If you can watch a video of a doctor go through the intricacies of an illness or injury, well, that would be quite helpful for many users. That video will bolster your site's credibility, and the products and services you offer on it.

Education related sites will also do quite well with videos. Many sites are putting someone up in front of a whiteboard with nothing more than a marker and some good ideas. Users like this, and they come back to watch future videos.

When visitors come by your site again and again they turn into users, and users are much more likely to turn into customers than just the casual visitor. Putting up videos that fill a need, answer a question, or just give good general knowledge that people didn't even know they needed will benefit your site long-term.

Counting

I've never been a big fan of math, but statistics enlighten me. They're easy to see, read, and they impart a lot of information quickly. The reason they do this is because they force us to associate things that we know with that number. If your site can claim it has 1,000,000 users or 1,000,000 products sold, that tells me a lot and it looks flashy. It gets my attention, and if that many people have given you their money, well, I better give you mine as well.

Statistics make us rely on logic, and the more you can put on the most important pages, the better your CRO will be for those pages. Another great way to use numbers on your site is to list how many people have bought that product, used that service, or looked at that blog. Counting up the numbers is great, and lots of people will compare you by your numbers. This might not work well if you're just starting out, but if you're really moving along with your site already, then it's something to think about.

Asking

No one wants to be badgered. Don't scare your visitors and potential customers away by asking for too much. You want their money or their attention, and you don't need a lot of information up front to get started on that. Visitors become users by getting onto your email list or by coming to your site everyday. You want to encourage them to do this, and all you really need is their email, username, and first name.

Try not to ask for more, and although some sites encourage users to enter more voluntarily, I frown on this. It's not a good idea because the longer someone has to fill in a form, the more likely they are to bounce from your site. Even seeing a form is enough to scare many users away unless they sought it out themselves. Keep it short, simple, and move them along.

The flip side of asking for too much is showing too much. Do you want to bombard your new user with ads? Do you know anyone who likes pop-up ads? And if you want someone to be a regular customer or user, do you need to display a large banner ad on that page? You're selling yourself here, not someone else's product. Scaring off a potential customer isn't worth those few pennies you'll get even if they click on your ad. Save those for other areas of your site that get a lot of random hits, like your home page or blog page.

26
WRITING A HOME PAGE

Why do I save writing a Home Page for last? Because I write books, and when I write books, I always do the introduction last. An introduction is really nothing more than a recap of all your book's chapters. And your website's Home Page is really nothing more than a good introduction to your website and its content.

Lots of people rush to put up a Home Page right when they get their website going. This is great, it gets you out there. But a lot of times you can scare those early visitors off with a poor Home Page design. And if you scare your early visitors off, they'll not become users.

The Good, the Bad, and the Ugly

I write a lot on the internet, and search out a lot of sites. For several months this year I've been writing about the wine industry, particularly in Australia. The Yarra Valley is a prime spot for wineries just outside of Melbourne, and I've visited at least 20 different winery websites.

Some of these sites are great; their content jumps out at you right away when you visit their Home Page. It's presented in a clear, concise, and easy-to-read format and it's certainly not taking up a lot of space. The sites which I found the most appealing had very little information below the fold of the page, which means I don't have to scroll down. Oftentimes the Home Page would only be one screen. Their links present the information that I need right away, and they're all presented clearly. By clicking on them I know where I'll be going.

Some of these winery websites are alright. Their content is a bit much, perhaps several long paragraphs. Still, if I read through it I'll get the information I'm looking for. Unfortunately, I've had to spend a few minutes reading a lot of stuff that doesn't interest me to find what does. These sites would do much better if they condensed their Home Page content, putting the details on their other pages. Many will also have lots of page that I have to scroll down. Some people might like this, but I don't. It tells me that the site is not organized properly and that a lot of thought hasn't gone into what content goes where.

And of course some of these sites are not so good. I don't want to say bad, but I might call them ugly. They do give me the information I'm looking for, it's just that I have to dig around to find it. Lots of content that should be on the About Us page is on the Home Page. Lots of product information is presented, which should probably only be given a link to the actual product pages.

The content is fluffy, tells me little in a lot of words, and oftentimes is poorly written. And don't even get me started on all the wild fonts, text colors, and background colors. Neon-colored text always gives me a headache, but for some reason people love to use it. Backgrounds with a similar color to the text also don't help me much, and might only increase my chances of needing an eye doctor soon.

And I can't tell you how many times I've seen wildly-sized fonts. Lots of times people think they can cram all the information they want into their Home Page if they just use an 8pt or 10pt font. If you're doing that I feel you're turning away many of your older internet users that might have an already difficult time seeing their screens; don't make it any harder on them than it already is.

These are all things that I see regularly, and which cause me to cringe. They make me want to hit the back button, and I often do. And that's when I'm getting paid to go to sites and check them out; imagine a regular internet user who's just surfing around. They'll hit back and have no qualms about it whatsoever.

Early Home Page Options

You can set your Home Page to any page on your website. A good place to do that is with your Blog. When you first get a new website up and running, write out a quick blog entry saying hello and what you intend with your new site. This blog comment will appear, but not for a long time like your Home Page will.

If you make new blog posts each day, it will go further and further down the page until no one looks at it at all anymore without searching through previous posts. And by typing up this short intro, you'll be making a great rough draft of what your Home Page content will contain.

When you've gotten your blog up and running, your content pages secure, and your product descriptions all cleared away, you can begin thinking about that Home Page. You've already got three bullet points right there:

- My Blog;
- My Content;
- My Products.

Put those into a bulleted list and talk about them on your Home Page. But remember; your Home Page shouldn't be cluttered, and most people aren't going to scroll too far down your page. If they do, it'll usually be just to see how long the page is.

Many people's eyes will also dart right over to your links, whether these are on a sidebar or up above. Those tell people a lot right there, and writing them should occupy some of your time, and thoughts. Simple things like: About Us, Products, Contact are all good. They're known the world over, and people know what to expect.

I've seen many sites where those same pages have different names, like: Our Story, Our Great Deals, and For More Info. Those tell you something, but perhaps they create more questions as well. It's probably better to stick with the known quantities until you've gotten your web presence secure and you know who your visitors are and where they're coming from. And there's a flip side to that as well. After all, if no one is visiting your Contact page, why not call it something else and see what happens? Perhaps that's all you need to do to finally get people clicking on it.

Remember, there are no firm rules for what works and what doesn't work on the internet. Things change quickly, and what's hot today in Home Pages could be so-last-year in a very short time. But just like men's suits, some things don't change that much over time. Simple and easy Home Page designs that you know and see regularly are what you want on your website.

Analyze the Competition

One of the best things you can do is find out what others are doing. Look at those popular websites you want to go up against, and scroll through the product descriptions on your toughest competitors. Analyze how clicking on search engine ads works, and what the different home and landing pages that are brought up look like.

You'll always learn more by seeing something yourself, and no book out there is going to give you the perfect design or answer. Look at your competition, but also allow your own style to flow through. Your visitors will be happy, you'll be happy, and both will allow you to continue creating and changing your great website..

ABOUT THE AUTHOR

Greg Strandberg was born and raised in Helena, Montana, and graduated from the University of Montana in 2008 with a BA in History. He lived and worked in China following the collapse of the American economy. After five years he moved back to Montana where he now lives with his wife and young son. He's written more than 50 books.

Connect with Greg Strandberg

http://www.bigskywords.com

Printed in Great Britain
by Amazon